READ ALOUD TALES of
INDIAN
MYTHOLOGY

Shiva - The Fisherman
and other stories...

Retold by

VANEETA VAID

Nita Mehta
Publications
Enriching Young Minds

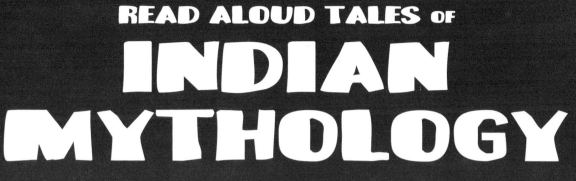

READ ALOUD TALES of
INDIAN MYTHOLOGY

Shiva - The Fisherman and other stories...

Nita Mehta
Publications
Enriching Young Minds

LARGE PRINT
READ ALOUD TALES of
INDIAN MYTHOLOGY
Shiva - The Fisherman
and other stories...

Distributed by :
NITA MEHTA BOOKS
3A/3, Asaf Ali Road, New Delhi - 02

Distribution Centre :
D16/1, Okhla Industrial Area, Phase-I,
New Delhi - 110020
Tel.: 26813199, 26813200
E-mail: nitamehta.mehta@gmail.com

Contributing Writers:
Subhash Mehta
Tanya Mehta

Editorial & Proofreading:
Rajesh
Ramesh

Nita Mehta Publications

Corporate Office
3A/3, Asaf Ali Road, New Delhi 110 002
Phone: +91 11 2325 2948, 2325 0091
Telefax: +91 11 2325 0091
E-mail: nitamehta@nitamehta.com
Website: www.nitamehta.com

First Print 2014

Printed in India at Infinity Advertising Services (P) Ltd, New Delhi

Editorial and Marketing office
E-159, Greater Kailash II, New Delhi 110 048

Typesetting by National Information Technology Academy
3A/3, Asaf Ali Road, New Delhi 110 002

Price: Rs. 145/-

CONTENTS

INTRODUCTION

Picked from the infinite treasury of legends emerging out of Indian mythology, these short stories represent the diverse formats of adventures, moral messages and the richness of the Indian style of story telling. The narratives are simple and involving, making sure that the readers do not lose their grip on the story line even for one moment.

THE BREAKING OF THE BOW

In the state of Mithila, King Janak announced that he was getting his daughter, princess Sita married.

King Janak put a condition to all the princes who had come to offer themselves as possible grooms.

Pointing to a huge bow, he said, "Sita will only marry the Prince who can lift and string this bow. The prince should then be able to snap the bow into two. This is lord Shiva's bow. This can only be strung and snapped by a god".

Why did King Janak put this condition? The reason being that Sita as a baby had lifted the bow easily. No one had been able to do that. Janak believed Sita to be an incarnation of goddess Lakshmi. Princes from far and wide tried to lift the bow. Alas! Not even one of them succeeded.

However, when the prince of Ayodhya, Prince Rama tried, *he not only lifted the bow but successfully strung it and broke it into two!* Prince Rama had fulfilled King Janak's condition.

The court bowed down to Rama. Shouts of, "Victory to Rama," erupted.

Suddenly, there was a commotion. Rishi Parshuram, the protector of all *rishis*, had arrived.

Wielding his axe, he threatened Rama, "How dare you break the bow that belonged to Shiva? I will kill you for it."

Prince Rama humbly reasoned with him. Parshuram was mollified. He was impressed with prince Rama's modesty. Since Rama had broken the bow, it was obvious that he too was the incarnation of a god. Prince Rama was believed to be the avatar of Lord Vishnu.

Happily, before long, a joyous marriage procession had reached Ayodhya with magnificently decorated chariots, horses, elephants and bullock carts.

Sita put a garland around Rama's neck and Rama and Sita were married. Along with them, Rama's three brothers married Sita's three sisters. The kingdom celebrated the happy event with much pomp and gaiety.

SHIVA - THE FISHERMAN

Lord Shiva angrily sent his wife Parvati away. He was, for some reason, very irritated with her. In anger he said, "Go and take birth as a fisher-woman on earth."

Parvati immediately disappeared!

Whatever Shiva wished for was bound to happen, you see.

Later, Shiva was very sorry he had uttered those words to Parvati.

"Oh no! I spoke without thinking," regretted Shiva.

Below on earth, Parvati was reborn as a baby girl. She was brought up by a fisherman and his wife.

Parvati grew up to be a very beautiful woman with a kind nature. She easily fitted into the fishing routines. She could expertly row boats and net fish.

From the heavens, Shiva sadly watched all this. He missed her very much. He knew that Parvati, being a fisher-woman was destined to marry only a fisherman.

Nandi, Shiva's attendant, decided to do something to get Shiva and Parvati back together again. He did not like the fact that Shiva was so sad.

Nandi descended on earth. He changed himself into a huge whale. He then swam into the same waters Parvati and her family fished.

Nandi as a whale, began to trouble the fishermen fishing there. He would bump into their boats, scare the fish, tear the nets or even chase the boats out of the surrounding areas.

The fishermen were scared to fish now. They ran to the temple and prayed to Lord Shiva to save them from the whale.

Parvati's father also announced that the fisherman who caught the whale would get Parvati's hand in marriage. Hearing this, all the eligible fisherman rushed to catch the whale. Nobody was successful though.

Shiva watching from above, decided to help. He changed himself into a fisherman. Lord Shiva arrived and presented himself to Parvati's father. He offered to net the whale. Parvati's father gave him permission.

We all know the whale was actually Nandi. Shiva had no problem netting him. The fishermen were overjoyed!

Soon, Shiva was reunited with Parvati. They returned to their abode and lived happily once again. Yes, not to forget Nandi. He was showered with praise and love from both Shiva and Parvati for his clever plan of bringing them back together again.

WHEN KRISHNA LIFTED MOUNT GOVERDHAN

Young Krishna was disturbed by Lord Indra's arrogant behaviour. Lord Indra was the god of thunder, lightening and rain.

With this thought in mind, Krishna asked the people of Brajdham to stop worshipping Indra.

Indra was furious on hearing this.

In revenge, he summoned the blackest of rain clouds and ordered them to rain in a deluge over Brajdham. Brajdham was under attack. Not by weapons but through rains accompanied by storms, lightening and thunder. The unending heavy rains grew into a natural calamity. The people of Brajdham were now battling a flood. Distressed, they begged Krishna to tell them what to do.

Krishna did not let them down. In front of many astonished eyes, he lifted the Govardhan Parvat, the largest mountain in the vicinity, in one heave. Holding the mountain high, on his little finger, he instructed everyone to take cover under it, as he held it up. The entire village found safe haven under the mountain Krishna held.

Soon, Lord Indra himself realized why Krishna had stopped people from praying to him.

Having understood Krishna's point, Indra instantly stopped the rains.

When the storms and rains were over, Lord Krishna asked the people to go back to their homes. Then he returned Govardhan Parvat to its original position.

THE BET

One day Arjun was challenged by a monkey to build a bridge of arrows. "I will step on to the bridge of arrows made by you and break it," proclaimed the monkey.

"That is not possible," Arjun exclaimed. Now every one knew that if Arjun made a bridge of arrows, he would a make a strong, unbreakable one. He was the king archer of those times and hated to be challenged.

"My bet says that if I cannot break your bridge of arrows, I will be declared your lifetime slave," said the monkey.

Arjun said, "Yes and if I lose, I will kill myself in a fire pyre."

"So be it," the monkey nodded.

Arjun sent out a barrage of arrows. With quick silver skill, he soon built a strong bridge.

With a confident stride, the monkey stepped on to the bridge.

WWWAAARRRRPPPPP! The bridge split into two; breaking almost instantly.

"I lose the challenge and accept the punishment," said Arjun.

Arjun lit a pyre. Suddenly, a boy materialized out of thin air.

The boy begged him to build one more bridge.

"Please continue the challenge. Let us see if this monkey can break the second bridge too."

Arjun agreed. He built another bridge.

This time the monkey could not break the bridge.

The monkey was actually Lord Hanuman. He had decided to test his strength against Arjun.

The second bridge did not break, in spite of Hanuman using all his strength.

Giving up, Hanuman stood next to Arjun.

Arjun turned to the little boy and fell to his knees,

"I know you are not an ordinary child."

The boy surveyed the two, then smiled. A huge mass of air rose before them. The boy was hidden completely. When the cloud cleared, Lord Vishnu stood before them.

"Arjun, you forgot to be humble. That is why Hanuman broke your bridge at first. As for you Hanuman, you became boastful. As a punishment, you will have to be on Arjun's flag pole all the time." Vishnu explained to them.

Hanuman and Arjun, sheepishly accepted Lord Vishnu's verdict.

THE DAY VISHNU BECOME AN ARROW

Three demon brothers, owned three separate flying cities. They had a boon from Brahma.

"I grant you such might that your cities cannot be destroyed. They can only be destroyed if they are struck by a single arrow. This arrow should be shot by a *divine archer*. The arrow can only strike when the cities are in one single line," said Brahma.

With this power, the three brothers created havoc in the heavens!

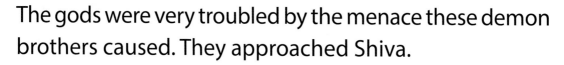

The gods were very troubled by the menace these demon brothers caused. They approached Shiva.

"Help us, dear Lord! Life in the heavens and earth is miserable because of these buoyant demon brothers with flying cities."

Shiva nodded, "I will help."

Thus, it was declared that Shiva was the chosen *divine archer*. Brahma was his charioteer.

Shiva waited for the cities to align in a single line in his exceptional chariot. His aim was to shoot them down with his bow and arrow.

Sadly Shiva was not successful, *because the cities never formed a single line and kept flying in different directions!*

"Listen, I have a plan," offered Vishnu. He took the form of a monk. He then visited the three cities. As a monk, Vishnu started to give lectures on existence. He slowly gained fame as a wise monk. The three demon brothers too heard of him. Right from the first lecture they heard, the brothers were mesmerized by the monk. They intently began to attend the wandering monk's sessions. Vishnu taught the demons the doctrine of releasing their soul from worldly goods. Eventually, the demons lost all interest in worldly life. They did not bother to fly their cities in different directions.

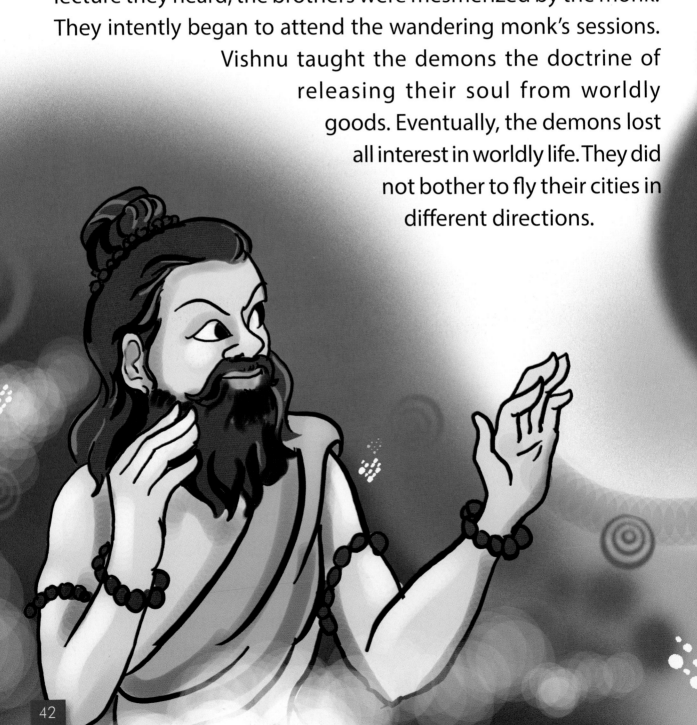

One day, when the demons were lulled into a deep meditation by Vishnu, the demons did not notice that the three cites lay in one single line. That is when Shiva struck!

Shiva drew his great bow. Do you know who was the arrow? None other than Vishnu himself ! Yes, Vishnu served as Shiva's arrow. Shiva twanged his bow. Vishnu hit all three cities, destroying them in an instant. Happiness returned to the heavens once again.

WORD GRID
FIND THE WORDS

A	W	S	H	I	V	A	P	Z	B
V	I	S	H	N	U	I	I	M	Q
N	K	Z	W	M	O	N	K	E	Y
Q	Z	I	B	O	W	K	L	S	T
Q	A	R	R	O	W	C	G	J	W
W	H	A	L	E	B	H	K	R	Z
T	H	K	N	M	D	E	M	O	N
G	L	W	B	K	I	N	G	F	G
R	G	H	P	A	R	V	A	T	I

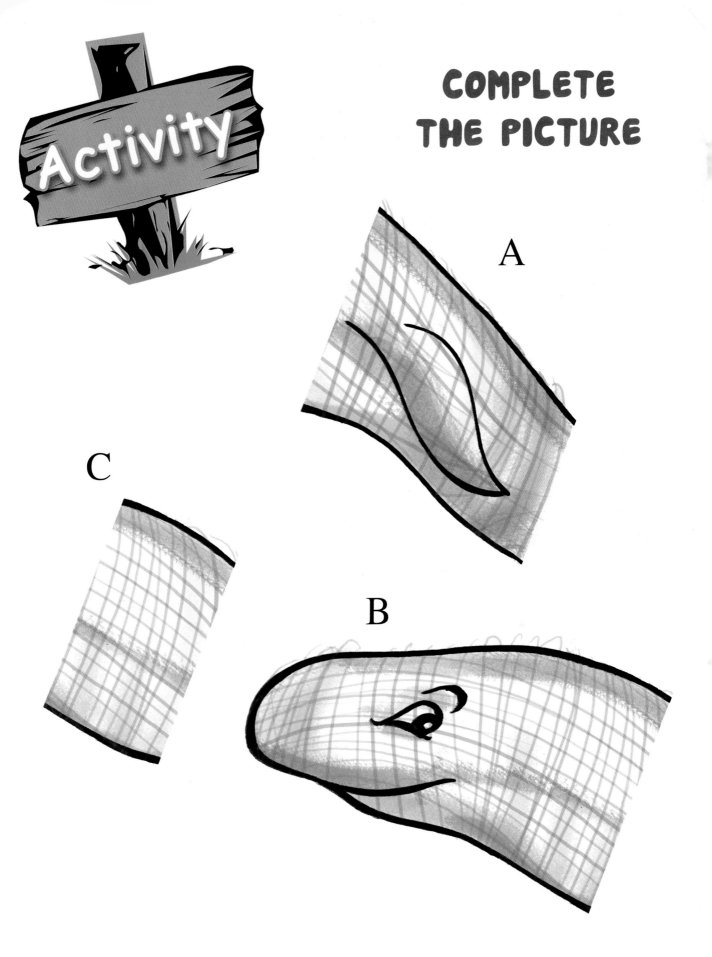

COMPLETE
THE PICTURE

A

C

B

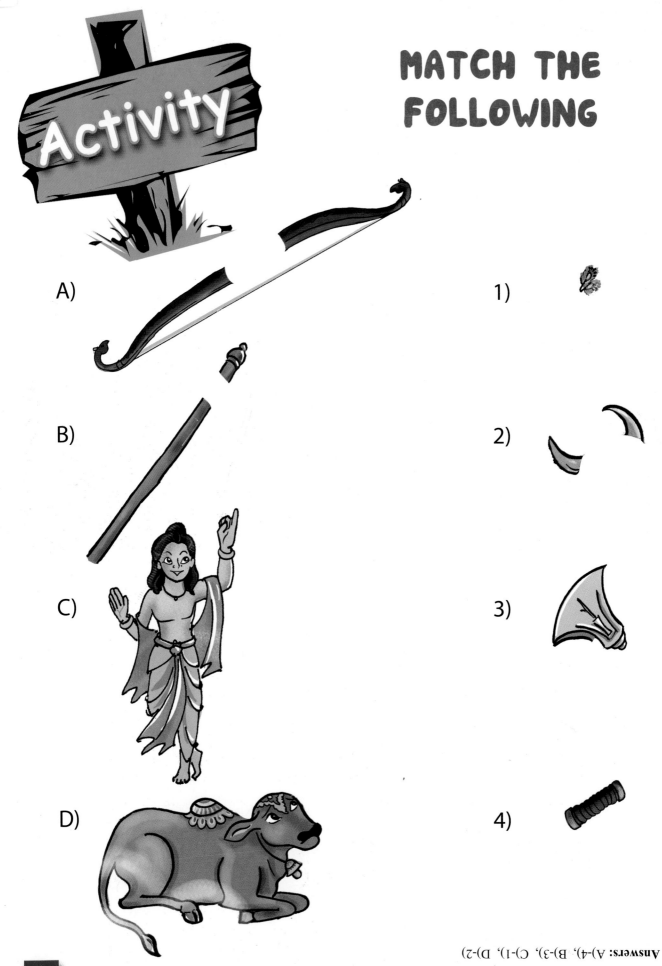

MATCH THE FOLLOWING

A)

B)

C)

D)

1)

2)

3)

4)

Answers: A)-4), B)-3), C)-1), D)-2)